D0791980

EYEWITNESS TO
THE ASSASSINATION OF ARCHDUKE FRANCIS FERDINAND

BY EMILY O'KEEFE

Published by The Child's World®
1980 Lookout Drive • Mankato, MN 56003-1705
800-599-READ • www.childsworld.com

Photographs ©: Heritage Images/The Print Collector/Glow Images, cover, 1; George Grantham Bain Collection/Library of Congress, 5; akg-images/Newscom, 6, 14, 17, 20; DEA/A. Dagli Orti/Getty Images, 8; Library of Congress, 10; Piepenburg/ullstein bild/ Getty Images, 13; The Print Collector Heritage Images/Newscom, 19; AP Images, 22; Superstock/Glow Images, 23; Everett Historical/Shutterstock Images, 24; PHOTOS.com/Thinkstock, 26

ISBN 9781503816039

LCCN 2016945649

Printed in the United States of America
PA02317

ABOUT THE AUTHOR

Emily O'Keefe is a writer and editor who enjoys learning about history, literature, and culture. She holds a PhD in English from Loyola University. O'Keefe lives in Chicago, Illinois.

TABLE OF
CONTENTS

Fast Facts..4

Chapter 1
A Visit to Bosnia.............................6

Chapter 2
The Archduke and the Emperor.......10

Chapter 3
The Black Hand 14

Chapter 4
The Assassination............................20

Chapter 5
The First World War 26

Think About It 29
Glossary 30
Source Notes 31
To Learn More 32
Index 32

FAST FACTS

Who was Francis Ferdinand?

- Francis Ferdinand was a member of the royal family in Austria-Hungary.
- Francis Ferdinand was an archduke, a position similar to that of a prince. He was the heir to the throne.

Where was Austria-Hungary?

- Austria-Hungary was in central Europe.
- The country was made up of parts of several modern countries. These countries include Austria, Hungary, Poland, Ukraine, Slovakia, Romania, Slovenia, Croatia, and Bosnia and Herzegovina.

Who assassinated Archduke Francis Ferdinand?

- Gavrilo Princip assassinated the archduke. Princip was a 19-year-old Bosnian man. He disagreed with Austria-Hungary's rule over Bosnia.

When was Francis Ferdinand assassinated?

- The archduke was assassinated on June 28, 1914.

Why was the assassination important?

- The assassination led to the start of World War I (1914–1918). Soon after the assassination, Austria-Hungary declared war on Serbia. **Allies** of both nations soon joined the war.

Chapter 1

A VISIT TO BOSNIA

On June 25, 1914, Archduke Francis Ferdinand arrived in Bosnia. His wife, Sophie, was beside him. Crowds welcomed the couple. Some people waved flags and offered flowers. Newspapers printed front-page articles about the visit. For days, the archduke and his wife explored the region. In each place, people gathered for a glimpse of the couple. Yet not everyone was glad about their arrival.

Francis Ferdinand was visiting Bosnia on official business for Austria-Hungary, a large empire in Europe. The archduke's uncle, Emperor Francis Joseph, led the country. Austria-Hungary included a variety of groups of people. These groups spoke different languages. They had different cultures. Bosnia had become part of Austria-Hungary in 1908. Most Bosnians were part of a group known as the Slavs. Many Slavs wanted to form their own nation. Some wanted to become part of Serbia, a nearby Slavic country. They did not like the archduke. Francis Ferdinand was part of the ruling Habsburg family. The Slavs blamed the Habsburgs for their lack of independence.

The archduke knew that his visit to Bosnia could be dangerous. Advisers had warned him to stay home. On the way to Bosnia, car troubles delayed the archduke's journey. He said the problems were a bad sign. Still, he was determined to make the trip. The archduke was known for his love of order and discipline. He had been invited to the Bosnian city of Sarajevo to attend military exercises. He would not let anything get in the way of his schedule.

The trip offered a rare chance for the archduke and Sophie to travel together. The couple had been married for nearly 14 years.

"By far the cleverest thing I ever did in my life was to marry my Sophie," said Francis Ferdinand.[1] However, his uncle had never approved of the match. Sophie was from a lower social class. The emperor thought she was an unsuitable wife. He forbade Sophie from attending events with her husband. But Bosnia was far away from the emperor's palace. Francis Ferdinand and Sophie were free to appear in public together. They sat side by side at important dinners. Officials greeted Sophie and gave her roses.

Francis Ferdinand and Sophie's wedding anniversary was on June 28, 1914. This was also the day of the main event in their trip. On that day, they would take a car trip together. They would travel through parts of Sarajevo. Then they would attend the military exercises.

Yet the journey did not happen as planned. Francis Ferdinand and Sophie never arrived. On their way, something terrible happened. It was an event that would change the world forever.

"Everything [is] fresh and lively. Tomorrow I shall visit Sarajevo and travel back in the evening."

—Francis Ferdinand, in a telegram on June 27, 1914[2]

◄ **Francis Ferdinand and Sophie were greeted warmly in Bosnia.**

Chapter 2

THE ARCHDUKE AND THE EMPEROR

In Ilidza, a small town outside of Sarajevo, officials greeted and honored Francis Ferdinand. On the evening of June 27, 1914, Francis Ferdinand hosted a dinner for 41 guests. The warm welcome was a change for Francis Ferdinand. For years at the palace in Vienna, Austria-Hungary's capital, he had been met with resistance.

◀ **Francis Joseph I had taken over Bosnia in 1908 after forming an unofficial agreement with Russia.**

At a royal dinner in 1913, Francis Ferdinand had warned others in the government of growing divisions in Austria-Hungary. Many Slavs had ties to Serbia. If they rebelled against Austria-Hungary, Serbia might support them. Francis Ferdinand raised his glass and proposed a toast to peace. "What would we get out of war with Serbia?" he went on to ask. "We'd lose the lives of young men and we'd spend money better used elsewhere."[3]

When Francis Joseph heard these remarks, he shook his head. The emperor believed in showing strength to other nations. Francis Joseph had led Austria-Hungary since it formed in 1867. Austria and Hungary had formed a **dual monarchy**. Both regions had separate governments. But the emperor had certain powers. He could **veto** laws passed by either government. He also had the power to declare war.

After years in power, the aging emperor disliked change. He refused to consider adjustments to the dual monarchy. But the arrangement gave power only to certain people. Slavs in Bosnia were one group with little power in the government. With time, Francis Ferdinand became convinced the empire needed to change. Otherwise, it faced the risk of rebellion and war.

In 1910, an assassin named Bogdan Zerajic fired shots at General Varesanin, the governor of Bosnia. The assassination attempt was unsuccessful. But it showed the growing tensions in the region.

Seeing these growing tensions, the archduke came up with ideas for changing Austria-Hungary. He believed more people should be allowed to vote. He also wanted to make areas of Austria-Hungary into states.

Francis Ferdinand hoped his proposals would help preserve peace. Yet Francis Joseph refused to listen to his nephew's warnings. If a war occurred, Francis Joseph planned to ask for help from allies. Kaiser Wilhelm II was the leader of Germany. He had vowed to assist Austria-Hungary in a crisis. "I stand behind you and am ready to draw the sword," he had promised.[4]

Francis Ferdinand spoke to military leaders, politicians, and others in the royal family about his ideas. Yet few were willing to consider his policies. Some thought the archduke was cold. Others were against his ideas for different reasons. Many ruling **elites** did not want to expand people's rights. Doing so could take away some of their own power.

Francis Ferdinand knew Francis Joseph would never agree with his proposals. But he was the heir to the throne. One day, he could have the power to change the empire.

In the meantime, Francis Ferdinand performed his duties as archduke. He made visits. He gave speeches. On June 28, 1914, he prepared for his visit to Sarajevo. He and Sophie would greet the people of the city.

▲ **Francis Ferdinand (left) met with Kaiser Wilhelm II (right) in 1913 to discuss tensions with Serbia.**

Chapter 3

THE BLACK HAND

As the archduke prepared for his visit to Sarajevo, another group was also making preparations: the Black Hand. The Black Hand was a secret Serbian organization. One of its goals was to free Slavs from Austria-Hungary's rule. The group often used violence to achieve its goals.

Earlier in June, three young men had snuck into Sarajevo. They carried weapons and plans.

The men traveled in secret, journeying through rough terrain. The Black Hand had recruited them and four others for a secret mission. The organization had trained the men to throw bombs and to fire guns. The men would join the crowds of people greeting the archduke. They would watch him ride through the streets of Sarajevo. Then they would attack.

The **conspirators** knew little about Francis Ferdinand. However, they knew he was part of the ruling Habsburg family. They believed that killing him would help bring freedom to the Slavic people.

Gavrilo Princip, a 19-year-old student, was one recruit. Princip had grown up in a poor Serbian family in western Bosnia. He had always been small and sickly. Yet, as a child, he was tough and eager to fight. "When playing, he was very rough," said his classmate Bozidar Tomic.[5] Later, Princip was rejected from a military unit due to his small size. The rejection deeply upset him. He wished to devote himself to a cause.

Apart from fighting, Princip enjoyed reading. Princip's family saw his eagerness to learn. They sent him away to study in Sarajevo. There he met classmates with **revolutionary** ideas. Princip began to oppose Austria-Hungary's control over Bosnia.

Many Slavic people in Bosnia were poor. It was difficult for them to buy land. Princip thought Slavs needed to fight for independence.

Like Princip, the other recruits were young. Trifko Grabez and Nedjelko Cabrinovic were also 19 years old. Grabez was the son of a priest. Cabrinovic had lived on his own since age 14. He had worked as a plumber, printer, and carpenter.

The men had led different lives. Yet their opinions were similar. They believed in independence for the Slavs through any way possible—even violence. This belief had brought them into contact with the Black Hand.

"I often spent whole nights . . . thinking about our situation, about our miserable conditions . . . and so it was that I resolved to carry out the assassination."

—*Gavrilo Princip*[6]

Princip, Grabez, and Cabrinovic met in Belgrade, Serbia, a center of revolutionary activity. One day, Cabrinovic received an envelope with no return address. Inside the envelope was a newspaper clipping.

Members of the Black Hand met at Ochrana Coffee House in ▶ Belgrade, Serbia.

The clipping talked about Francis Ferdinand's planned visit to Bosnia. Cabrinovic shared the clipping with Princip and Grabez.

That envelope was the beginning of the plot to assassinate Francis Ferdinand. Most likely, a member of the Black Hand had sent the clipping to Cabrinovic. Serbian army officials had formed the Black Hand in 1911. By 1914, the group had hundreds of members. They planned to create what they called Greater Serbia. This land would include the nation of Serbia. It would also include Slavic parts of Austria-Hungary. Members of the Black Hand believed the assassination would help them take control of these Slavic areas. Soon, they began training the young men to carry out the assassination.

The Black Hand's activities were secret. Members did not speak openly about the group. Still, the organization was a powerful force in Serbia. Many government officials were part of it. The prime minister, Nikola Pasic, was not a member. Yet he knew about many of the group's activities. By early June 1914, he had learned about the plot to assassinate Francis Ferdinand.

Pasic feared the effects of the plot. He believed it could lead to war. He sent a Serbian official to warn against the archduke's trip. The official spoke to Leon von Bilinski, Austria's minister of finance. "Some young Serb might put a . . . **cartridge** in his gun and fire it," he cautioned.[7]

▲ **The Black Hand was displeased with Serbian prime minister Nikola Pasic for not using force for the Serbian cause.**

Bilinski misunderstood the seriousness of the warning. "Let us hope nothing does happen," he responded.[8] The archduke's trip to Sarajevo went ahead as planned. The seven conspirators gathered their supplies. They carried four pistols and six bombs. They prepared to meet Francis Ferdinand.

Chapter 4

THE ASSASSINATION

June 28, 1914, was a sunny day in Sarajevo. In the morning, Francis Ferdinand and Sophie got into an open-topped car called a Phaeton. It was one of the first of its kind. From the car, they could see the crowds on the streets. They could wave to the people who were gathered to see them.

The couple was dressed in fine clothing. Francis Ferdinand wore a blue and gold uniform.

Sophie wore a white dress and veil. She carried a bouquet of roses. Before the couple left, a photographer snapped their picture.

The archduke's **motorcade** began its journey. The planned route had been published in advance. People crowded along the streets. Some leaned in to catch a glimpse. Local residents unfurled flags from their windows. A small number of police officers stood watch. Within the crowds, the conspirators waited. They had split up to cover more ground. The seven men took their positions along the route.

The first attack occurred at 10:10 a.m. The crowd screamed as Cabrinovic threw a bomb at the motorcade. Acting quickly, the driver accelerated. The bomb missed Francis Ferdinand. It exploded beneath the car with a loud noise. Shattered glass and **debris** wounded several people. At first, Francis Ferdinand reacted calmly. He rejected suggestions to return home. "Come on, that fellow is clearly insane," he said. "Let us proceed with our program."[9]

Francis Ferdinand and Sophie stopped at city hall. The mayor of Sarajevo welcomed them to the city. But the bombing had shaken the couple. After the speech, they rethought their plans.

They would not stay in Sarajevo, after all. Advisers agreed the original plan would be too risky. Instead, the couple would go to the hospital and visit the people hurt by the bomb.

Francis Ferdinand and Sophie entered their car. But the driver was unaware of the new plan. He set out on the original route. "You're going the wrong way!" one general yelled, frantically.[10]

▲ **Francis Ferdinand and Sophie leave city hall after meeting with the mayor of Sarajevo.**

▲ **Francis Ferdinand and Sophie were unprotected in the open-topped car.**

The driver hastily tapped the brake. Nearby, Princip was standing in front of a café. The car stopped only 5 feet (1.5 m) away from him.

When the car halted, Princip saw his chance. The assassin stepped forward while retrieving a pistol from his pocket. He fired the pistol twice. One shot hit Francis Ferdinand and the other hit Sophie. A commotion erupted in the motorcade.

At first, others in the car did not know what had happened. As Sophie slumped forward, the others helped her up.

They believed Sophie had fainted, but as blood began to trickle from Francis Ferdinand's mouth, they began to realize what had happened.

The car rushed them to the house of Oskar Potiorek, the governor of Bosnia. "Stay alive, Sophie, for the sake of the children!" Francis Ferdinand pleaded to his wife.[11] But it was too late. Within an hour, the archduke and Sophie had died from their wounds.

> "We have profound regrets . . . we did not know that the late [Francis] Ferdinand was a father."
>
> —Nedjelko Cabrinovic, during his trial[12]

Meanwhile, a shocked crowd surrounded Princip. People pushed the assassin and knocked the gun from his hands. Police officers captured Princip and led him away. They had already caught Cabrinovic. The men would later be sentenced to jail time.

News of the assassination spread. Political leaders debated what to do. The assassin had been caught. But politicians knew Princip had not acted alone. Many suspected the Serbian government had supported the plot. They vowed to take revenge.

◀ **Officials arrest a suspect following the first attack on Francis Ferdinand and Sophie.**

Chapter 5

THE FIRST WORLD WAR

Around the world, people reacted to the tragic event in Sarajevo.
Governments across Europe announced periods of mourning.
A French newspaper called the assassination "a European event of
the highest political importance."[13] Yet few could have predicted
what would happen next.

◄ **After a procession through Vienna, the couple's funeral took place on July 3, 1914.**

In Sarajevo, authorities questioned the conspirators. They wanted to know whether Serbia was behind the attack. Princip insisted the conspirators had acted alone. "The idea arose in our own minds," he later claimed. "We ourselves executed it."[14] Francis Joseph and his advisers did not believe Princip. Many urged strong action against Serbia. Even Francis Ferdinand's enemies wanted revenge. Some had long wanted to go to war with Serbia. They used Francis Ferdinand's death as an excuse to act.

Francis Joseph's advisers began to prepare for war. The emperor himself was unsure at first whether to lead Austria-Hungary into conflict. He wanted to know he had Germany's support. He sent a letter to Kaiser Wilhelm II shortly after the assassination. On July 6, he received his answer. The Kaiser vowed to "faithfully stand by Austria-Hungary."[15] Germany would support its ally, no matter what the country decided.

Some cautioned that a war could be disastrous. The prime minister of Hungary, Istvan Tisza, had spoken against angering Serbia. Russia was Serbia's ally. France and the United Kingdom were allies of Russia. Tisza thought these countries might fight to defend Serbia. A conflict could become a *Weltkrieg*, or world war.

Tisza was shocked to hear about the assassination. He wondered whether his fears were coming true. Would Austria-Hungary start a war? Other nations would soon join the conflict. It could be the most destructive war in history.

On July 7, Tisza joined a meeting of the Crown Council. This was a group of advisers to the emperor. The other four members of the council supported an immediate attack on Serbia. Oskar Potiorek, the governor of Bosnia, said only "the sword" could resolve their dispute.[16] Eventually, Tisza convinced the council to compromise. Austria-Hungary would produce a list of demands for Serbia. If Serbia did not meet the demands, the emperor would declare war.

The demands were strict. Serbia would need to remove all groups similar to the Black Hand from the country. It would have to let Austria-Hungary investigate the assassination. That would mean investigating the Serbian government.

"You will be home before the leaves have fallen from the trees."

—Kaiser Wilhelm II, speaking to soldiers. Most Europeans expected only a short war.[17]

On July 23, Austria-Hungary gave Serbia an **ultimatum**. Serbia needed to agree to the demands in 48 hours. If it did not, Austria-Hungary would declare war. Serbia met most but not all of the demands. Prime Minister Pasic urged for more discussion. Leaders of Austria-Hungary refused. On July 28, 1914, Francis Joseph declared war. He announced the decision in a poster. Copies of the poster told the public about the war. Exactly one month had passed since Francis Ferdinand's death.

Days later, Germany and Russia entered the war. Other countries soon followed: France, the United Kingdom, and Japan. Most declared war to support their allies. Soon, the violent conflict would affect people everywhere. A world war had begun.

THINK ABOUT IT

- Francis Ferdinand did not want to go to war with Serbia. If he had lived, would a world war still have happened? Why or why not?
- Francis Ferdinand and his uncle, Francis Joseph, disagreed about many ideas. How were they different?
- How are alliances between countries dangerous? Did alliances make conflicts in Europe worse? Why or why not?

GLOSSARY

allies (AL-eyes): Allies are countries that are united by an agreement. Sometimes, allies agree to fight on the same side during a war.

cartridge (KAR-trij): A cartridge is a small cylinder that contains a bullet and an explosive material. A cartridge is fired with a gun.

conspirators (kun-SPEER-uh-terz): Conspirators are people who take part in a secret plot. Conspirators plotted to kill Francis Ferdinand.

debris (duh-BREE): Debris contains ruins or broken-down objects. The bomb thrown at the archduke's car created debris.

dual monarchy (DOO-ul MON-ar-kee): A dual monarchy is a union of two nations in which one leader has power over both. Austria-Hungary was a dual monarchy ruled by Francis Joseph.

elites (ih-LEETS): Elites are people with the most power or highest class in a particular nation or society. In Austria-Hungary, elites included politicians and generals.

motorcade (MO-tar-kade): A motorcade is a group of cars that move together in a line. A world leader or politician might travel in a motorcade.

revolutionary (rev-uh-LOO-shun-air-ee): A revolutionary idea is one that involves a complete change of a nation's leadership. The Black Hand held revolutionary ideas.

ultimatum (ul-tuh-MAY-tum): An ultimatum is a threat or a final demand. Austria-Hungary gave an ultimatum to Serbia to agree to its demands or to face war.

veto (VEE-toh): To veto a decision means to stop it from becoming law. The emperor could veto measures passed by the governments of Austria and Hungary.

SOURCE NOTES

1. Talia Mindich. "Eight Things You Didn't Know about Franz Ferdinand." *PBS NewsHour.* NewsHour Productions, 27 Jun. 2014. Web. 8 Apr. 2015.

2. T. G. Otte. *July Crisis: The World's Descent into War, Summer 1914.* Cambridge, UK: Cambridge UP, 2014. Print. 23.

3. Frederic Morton. *Thunder at Twilight: Vienna 1913/1914.* Boston, MA: Da Capo, 2014. Print. 37.

4. "Beginning the Great War." *Fifteen Eighty-Four.* Cambridge UP, 2 Jul. 2014. Web. 15 Apr. 2016.

5. Tony Fabijancic. *Bosnia: In the Footsteps of Gavrilo Princip.* Calgary, AB: U of Alberta Press, 2010. Print. 13.

6. Richard Preston. "First World War Centenary: The Assassination of Franz Ferdinand as It Happened." *Telegraph.* Telegraph Media Group, 27 Jun. 2014. Web. 8 Apr. 2015.

7. Michael Shackelford. "Sarajevo, June 28, 1914." *World War I Document Archive.* Brigham Young University, n.d. Web. 18 Apr. 2016.

8. Ibid.

9. Richard Preston. "First World War Centenary: The Assassination of Franz Ferdinand as It Happened." *Telegraph.* Telegraph Media Group, 27 Jun. 2014. Web. 8 Apr. 2015.

10. Ari Shapiro. "A Century Ago in Sarajevo: A Plot, a Farce, and a Fateful Shot." *NPR.* NPR, 27 Jun. 2014. Web. 7 Apr. 2016.

11. Ibid.

12. "Cabrinovic, Nedjelko." *World War I Document Archive.* Brigham Young University, n.d. Web. 18 Apr. 2016.

13. Richard Preston. "First World War Centenary: The Assassination of Franz Ferdinand as It Happened." *Telegraph.* Telegraph Media Group, 27 Jun. 2014. Web. 8 Apr. 2015.

14. "The 'Blank Check.'" *World War I Document Archive.* Brigham Young University, n.d. Web. 18 Apr. 2016.

15. "Gavrilo Princip." *World War I Document Archive.* Brigham Young University, n.d. Web. 18 Apr. 2016.

16. Gordon Martel. *July 1914: The Month That Changed the World.* Oxford, UK: Oxford UP, 2014. Print. 120.

17. "Germany and France Declare War on Each Other." *History.* A&E Networks, 2016. Web. 15 Apr. 2016.

TO LEARN MORE

Books

Adams, Simon. *World War I*. New York: DK, 2014.

Bearce, Stephanie. *World War I: Spies, Secret Missions, and Hidden Facts from World War I*. Waco, TX: Prufrock, 2014.

Kenney, Karen Latchana. *Everything World War I*. Washington, DC: National Geographic, 2014.

Web Sites

Visit our Web site for links about Archduke Francis Ferdinand: childsworld.com/links

Note to Parents, Teachers, and Librarians: We routinely verify our Web links to make sure they are safe and active sites. So encourage your readers to check them out!

INDEX

allies, 5, 12, 28–29

assassin, 12, 23, 25

Austria-Hungary, 4–5, 7, 11–12, 15–16, 18, 27–29

Bilinski, Leon von, 18–19

Black Hand, 14–18, 28

Bosnia, 4, 7–9, 12, 15–16

Cabrinovic, Nedjelko, 16–18, 21, 25

conspirators, 15, 18–19, 21, 25, 27

Crown Council, 28

dual monarchy, 11

France, 27, 29

Francis Joseph, 7, 11–12, 27, 29

Germany, 12, 27–29

Grabez, Trifko, 16–18

Greater Serbia, 18

Habsburgs, 7, 15

Japan, 29

motorcade, 21, 23

Pasic, Nikola, 18, 29

Potiorek, Oskar, 25, 28

Princip, Gavrilo, 4, 15–18, 23–25, 27

Russia, 27–29

Serbia, 5, 7, 11, 15–16, 18–19, 25, 27–29

Sophie, 6, 7–9, 13, 20–25

Tisza, Istvan, 27–28

Tomic, Bozidar, 15

ultimatum, 29

United Kingdom, 27, 29

Weltkrieg, 27

Wilhelm II, 12, 27–28

Zerajic, Bogdan, 12